TO ME

김민준

1990년 7월 8일 마산에서 태어났다. 민족문학작가회의 경남청소년문학대상에서 대상을 받으며 글 재능을 인정받았다. 한양대학교 신문방송학과에 재학 중, 인스타그램에 올린 글들이 입소문을 타고 좋은 반응을 이끌며 SNS 인기 작가로 유명해지기 시작했다. 그 글들을 독립출판물로 엮어 『추억으로 남기려거든 반드시 한 걸음 물러설 것』을 펴냈다. 현재 팟캐스트 '그 남자의 방'에서 책과 영화를 통한 삶의 희망과 사랑을 이야기하고 있다. 지은 책으로 『계절에서 기다릴게』, 『니 생각』이 있다.

팟캐스트 http://www.podbbang.com/ch/9059
인스타그램 http://instagram.com/mjmjmorning

"Q&A
TO ME
나를 찾아 떠나는 1000일
"

프로젝트A

Q&A To Me
나를 찾아가는 1000일의 기록

오늘은 결국에 어제가 된다.
시간이 너를 위로하고 있다.
— 계절에서 기다릴게 중에서

우리가 무언가를 기록하는 이유는 어제와 오늘, 그리고
다가올 내일 사이에서 방황하지 않고 굳건히 나의 길을 가기 위함입니다.
이곳은 지극히 사적인 공간, 앞으로 경험하는 모든 감정의 종착역은
지금, 여기, 이 순간이 될 것입니다.

그저 스치며 지나기엔 아쉬운 오늘을 기록해 보세요.
1,000일 동안의 내 감정 변화를 바라보며
스스로 얼마나 성장했는지 깨닫게 될 겁니다.

How to...

1.
오늘의 나를 자유롭고 생생하게 기록합니다.
누군가에게 보일 것을 염두에 두지 않고 기록하기를 권장합니다.
그리고 마치 영상을 서술하듯 되도록 자세하게 적습니다.
그러면 이 한 권의 책은 생생한 자기보고서가 되어 줄 것입니다.

2.
정답은 없습니다. 수려한 문장으로 기록하려고 노력하지 마세요.
그저 나의 기억과 마음을 솔직하게 기록하면 됩니다.
그리고 기록에는 정해진 순서가 없습니다.
질문을 훑어보며 마음이 가는 질문을 펼쳐 답변을 기록하면 됩니다.

3.
한 질문에 대하여 세 번의 답변을 넣도록 구성되어 있습니다.
시간의 흐름에 따라 달라진 생각을 한 페이지 안에서 비교할 수 있습니다.
그 단위는 꼭 1년의 흐름이 아니어도 상관없습니다.
하지만 날짜를 기재하는 것은 잊지 마세요.

4.
첫 번째 질문은 책을 펼치고 가장 우선으로 작성합니다.
그리고 나머지 빈 공간을 자유롭게 채워갑니다.

경험을 현명하게 사용한다면,
어떤 일도 시간 낭비는 아니다

—

오귀스트 르네 로댕

1
Steps towards the dream

★

나는 누구인가?

_____ year _____ month _____ day

2*3*4
Steps towards the dream

★

나는 어릴 적 어떤 꿈을 꾸었나?

_____ year _____ month _____ day

_____ year _____ month _____ day

_____ year _____ month _____ day

5*6*7

Steps towards the dream

★

펼치지 못한 나의 꿈들은 무엇이 있을까?

_____ year _____month _____day

_____ year _____month _____day

_____ year _____month _____day

8*9*10

Steps towards the dream

★

한계에 부딪힌 경험이 있었는가?

_____ year _____month _____day

_____ year _____month _____day

_____ year _____month _____day

11*12*13

Steps towards the dream

★

아직도 잊혀지지 않는 사랑이 있는가?

_____ year _____month _____day

_____ year _____month _____day

_____ year _____month _____day

14*15*16
Steps towards the dream

★

타인에게 나는 어떤 사람으로 기억되고 싶은가?

_____ year _____ month _____ day

_____ year _____ month _____ day

_____ year _____ month _____ day

17*18*19

Steps towards the dream

★

내가 지금 하고 있는 일은 무엇인가?

_____ year _____month _____day

_____ year _____month _____day

_____ year _____month _____day

20*21*22

Steps towards the dream

★

오늘 하루, 감사했던 일들이 있는가?

_____ year _____month _____day

_____ year _____month _____day

_____ year _____month _____day

23*24*25

Steps towards the dream

★

내일의 나는 어떤 모습일까?

_____ year _____month _____day

_____ year _____month _____day

_____ year _____month _____day

26*27*28

Steps towards the dream

★

3년 후의 나에게 해주고 싶은 말은 무엇인가?

_____ year _____month _____day

_____ year _____month _____day

_____ year _____month _____day

진정한 삶이란

작은 변화들의 모였을 때 나타납니다.

—

레프 톨스토이

29*30*31
Steps towards the dream

★

나를 슬프게 했던 일은 어떤 것이었나?

_____ year _____month _____day

_____ year _____month _____day

_____ year _____month _____day

32*33*34

Steps towards the dream

★

나만의 오래된 습관은 무엇인가?

_____ year _____month _____day

_____ year _____month _____day

_____ year _____month _____day

35*36*37
Steps towards the dream

내가 좋아하는 공간은 어떤 곳인가?

_____ year _____month _____day

_____ year _____month _____day

_____ year _____month _____day

38*39*40

Steps towards the dream

★

내가 추구하는 삶은 어떠한 삶인가?

_____ year _____month _____day

_____ year _____month _____day

_____ year _____month _____day

41*42*43

Steps towards the dream

★

나를 가장 잘 표현할 수 있는 단어는?

_____ year _____month _____day

_____ year _____month _____day

_____ year _____month _____day

44*45*46

Steps towards the dream

★

꼭 해야 하는데 미루고 있는 일이 있다면?

_____ year _____ month _____ day

_____ year _____ month _____ day

_____ year _____ month _____ day

47*48*49

Steps towards the dream

★

오늘 이후, 스스로의 다짐이 있다면?

_____ year _____month _____day

_____ year _____month _____day

_____ year _____month _____day

50*51*52

Steps towards the dream

★

두려움을 극복해본 경험이 있는가?

_____ year _____month _____day

_____ year _____month _____day

_____ year _____month _____day

53*54*55

Steps towards the dream

★

내가 좋아하는 것들의 공통된 특징은 무엇인가?

_____ year _____month _____day

_____ year _____month _____day

_____ year _____month _____day

56*57*58

Steps towards the dream

★

지금보다 더 나은 미래를 위해 해야 할 일은 무엇이 있을까?

_____ year _____month _____day

_____ year _____month _____day

_____ year _____month _____day

그림자가 있는 곳에는 반드시 밝은 빛이 있다.
—
레프 톨스토이

59*60*61
Steps towards the dream

★

과거에는 소중했으나
지금은 의미없이 느껴지는 것은 무엇이 있을까?

_____ year _____ month _____ day

_____ year _____ month _____ day

_____ year _____ month _____ day

Steps towards the dream

★

돌아가고 싶은 순간이 있다면 언제인가?

_____ year _____ month _____ day

_____ year _____ month _____ day

_____ year _____ month _____ day

Steps towards the dream

가장 기억에 남는 첫 경험은 무엇인가?

_____ year _____month _____day

_____ year _____month _____day

_____ year _____month _____day

68*69*70
Steps towards the dream

★

내가 히어로가 된다면 어떤 캐릭터가 좋을까?

_____ year _____ month _____ day

_____ year _____ month _____ day

_____ year _____ month _____ day

71*72*73
Steps towards the dream

내 삶의 원동력은 무엇인가?

_____ year _____month _____day

_____ year _____month _____day

_____ year _____month _____day

74*75*76
Steps towards the dream

★

나는 나를 사랑하는가?

_____ year _____month _____day

_____ year _____month _____day

_____ year _____month _____day

77*78*79

Steps towards the dream

★

내가 가장 부러워하는 대상은 누구인가?

___ year ___ month ___ day

___ year ___ month ___ day

___ year ___ month ___ day

80*81*82

Steps towards the dream

★

노력이 상황을 바꿀 수 있을까?

_____ year _____month _____day

_____ year _____month _____day

_____ year _____month _____day

83*84*85
Steps towards the dream

★

능력 있는 사람이란 어떤 사람일까?

_____ year _____month _____day

_____ year _____month _____day

_____ year _____month _____day

86*87*88
Steps towards the dream

★

성공이란 무엇을 의미하는가?

_____ year _____ month _____ day

_____ year _____ month _____ day

_____ year _____ month _____ day

인간은 분수와 같다. 분자는 자신의 실제이며
분모는 자신에 대한 평가이다.
분모가 클수록 분수는 작아진다.

―

레프 톨스토이

89*90*91

Steps towards the dream

★

나는 앞으로 어떤 사랑을 하고 싶은가?

_____ year _____month _____day

_____ year _____month _____day

_____ year _____month _____day

92*93*94

Steps towards the dream

★

내 첫 사랑에 대한 기억은 어떤 감정일까?

_____ year _____ month _____ day

_____ year _____ month _____ day

_____ year _____ month _____ day

95*96*97

Steps towards the dream

★

지금, 생각나는 장소는 어디인가?

_____ year _____month _____day

_____ year _____month _____day

_____ year _____month _____day

98*99*100
Steps towards the dream

사랑하는 사람에게 듣고 싶은 말은 무엇인가?

_____ year _____month _____day

_____ year _____month _____day

_____ year _____month _____day

101*102*103
Steps towards the dream

★

누군가에게 하지 못한 말이 있다면 무엇인가?

_____ year _____month _____day

_____ year _____month _____day

_____ year _____month _____day

104*105*106
Steps towards the dream

★

타인을 배려하는 것은 나에게 어떤 의미인가?

_____ year _____month _____day

_____ year _____month _____day

_____ year _____month _____day

107*108*109
Steps towards the dream

★

가장 행복했던 시절의 나와 오늘의 나는 무엇이 다른가?

_____ year _____month _____day

_____ year _____month _____day

_____ year _____month _____day

110*111*112
Steps towards the dream

★

나는 완벽주의자인가?

_____ year _____month _____day

_____ year _____month _____day

_____ year _____month _____day

113*114*115
Steps towards the dream

★

내게 부족한 것은 무엇인가?

_____ year _____month _____day

_____ year _____month _____day

_____ year _____month _____day

116*117*118
Steps towards the dream

★

나는 지금, 노력하고 있는가?

_____ year _____month _____day

_____ year _____month _____day

_____ year _____month _____day

좋은 일을 하려고 노력하기 보다는
오히려 좋은 인간이 되도록 노력해야 한다

—

레프 톨스토이

119*120*121
Steps towards the dream

★

나는 언제 화가 나는가?

_____ year _____month _____day

_____ year _____month _____day

_____ year _____month _____day

122*123*124
Steps towards the dream

★

타인의 시선을 신경 쓰는 때는 언제인가?

_____ year _____month _____day

_____ year _____month _____day

_____ year _____month _____day

125*126*127
Steps towards the dream

★

내게 혼자 있는 시간은 어떤 의미인가?

_____ year _____month _____day

_____ year _____month _____day

_____ year _____month _____day

128*129*130
Steps towards the dream

★

일을 마친 후 나는 무슨 생각을 하는가?

_____ year _____month _____day

_____ year _____month _____day

_____ year _____month _____day

131*132*133

Steps towards the dream

★

내가 좋아하는 노랫말은 무엇인가?

_____ year _____ month _____ day

_____ year _____ month _____ day

_____ year _____ month _____ day

134*135*136
Steps towards the dream

★

가장 행복했던 시간은 언제인가?

_____ year _____ month _____ day

_____ year _____ month _____ day

_____ year _____ month _____ day

137*138*139

Steps towards the dream

★

가까운 주변인들은 나를 어떤 사람이라고 말하는가?

_____ year _____month _____day

_____ year _____month _____day

_____ year _____month _____day

140*141*142
Steps towards the dream

★

행복이란 무엇인가?

___ year ___month ___day

___ year ___month ___day

___ year ___month ___day

가장 위대하고 심오한 진리는
가장 단순하고 소박합니다.

—

레프 톨스토이

Steps towards the dream

★

일상이 지루하고 따분하게 느껴진다면 왜일까?

_____ year _____ month _____ day

_____ year _____ month _____ day

_____ year _____ month _____ day

146*147*148
Steps towards the dream

★

나를 즐겁게 하는 것들은 무엇인가?

_____ year _____month _____day

_____ year _____month _____day

_____ year _____month _____day

149*150*151
Steps towards the dream

★

무언가를 포기하지 않고 꾸준히 행한 적이 있는가?

_____ year _____month _____day

_____ year _____month _____day

_____ year _____month _____day

152*153*154
Steps towards the dream

★

내게 스마트 폰이란 어떤 의미인가?

_____ year _____ month _____ day

_____ year _____ month _____ day

_____ year _____ month _____ day

155*156*157
Steps towards the dream

★

계획을 이루지 못했다면 이유는 무엇일까?

_____ year _____month _____day

_____ year _____month _____day

_____ year _____month _____day

158*159*160
Steps towards the dream

★

성취감을 느꼈던 일은 어떤 일이었는가?

_____ year _____month _____day

_____ year _____month _____day

_____ year _____month _____day

161*162*163
Steps towards the dream

지금까지의 인생에서 가장 고된 시련은 언제인가?

_____ year _____month _____day

_____ year _____month _____day

_____ year _____month _____day

164*165*166

Steps towards the dream

★

1년 전의 나는 오늘의 나와 무엇이 달라져 있는가?

_____ year _____ month _____ day

_____ year _____ month _____ day

_____ year _____ month _____ day

167*168*169
Steps towards the dream

★

오늘의 나에게 하고 싶은 말은 무엇인가?

_____ year _____ month _____ day

_____ year _____ month _____ day

_____ year _____ month _____ day

Steps towards the dream

★

나에게 탈선이란 어떤 행위를 말하는가?

_____ year _____month _____day

_____ year _____month _____day

_____ year _____month _____day

욕망은 처음에 문을 열어 달라고 간청하다가
어느덧 손님이 되고 곧 마음의 주인이 된다.

—

레프 톨스토이

173*174*175
Steps towards the dream

★

나는 언제 외로운가?

_____ year _____month _____day

_____ year _____month _____day

_____ year _____month _____day

Steps towards the dream

★

혼자서 할 수 있는 일은 무엇이 있는가?

_____ year _____month _____day

_____ year _____month _____day

_____ year _____month _____day

179*180*181
Steps towards the dream

★

오늘 아침, 점심, 저녁 메뉴는 무엇인가?

_____ year _____month _____day

_____ year _____month _____day

_____ year _____month _____day

182*183*184
Steps towards the dream

★

유대관계를 잘 유지하는 방법은 무엇일까?

_____ year _____month _____day

_____ year _____month _____day

_____ year _____month _____day

185*186*187

Steps towards the dream

★

타인과 다른 독특한 특징이 나에게 있는가?

_____ year _____month _____day

_____ year _____month _____day

_____ year _____month _____day

188*189*190
Steps towards the dream

★

친한 친구에게 하고 싶은 따뜻한 말 한마디는 무엇인가?

_____ year _____month _____day

_____ year _____month _____day

_____ year _____month _____day

191*192*193
Steps towards the dream

★

내가 우울할 때 위로받을 수 있는 것들은 무엇이 있는가?

_____ year _____ month _____ day

_____ year _____ month _____ day

_____ year _____ month _____ day

194*195*196

Steps towards the dream

★

혼자 떠나고 싶은 여행지가 있는가?

_____ year _____month _____day

_____ year _____month _____day

_____ year _____month _____day

197*198*199

Steps towards the dream

★

요즘 내가 가장 많이 하는 생각은 무엇인가?

_____ year _____month _____day

_____ year _____month _____day

_____ year _____month _____day

200*201*202

Steps towards the dream

★

누구와, 언제, 어디서, 무엇을, 왜, 어떻게 떠나고 싶은가?

_____ year _____month _____day

_____ year _____month _____day

_____ year _____month _____day

길을 걸어가려면 자신이 어디로 향하고 있는지를 알아야 한다.
합리적이고 선량한 생활을 영위하려는 경우도 마찬가지다.
자신과 타인의 생활을 어디로 이끌어 가고 있는지 알아야 한다.

―

레프 톨스토이

203*204*205

Steps towards the dream

★

오늘 들었던 말들은 무엇인가?

_____ year _____month _____day

_____ year _____month _____day

_____ year _____month _____day

206*207*208

Steps towards the dream

★

오늘 겪었던 일 중 가장 평범하지 않은 일은 무엇인가?

_____ year _____month _____day

_____ year _____month _____day

_____ year _____month _____day

209*210*211
Steps towards the dream

★

지금 당장 하고 싶은 것은 무엇인가?

_____ year _____ month _____ day

_____ year _____ month _____ day

_____ year _____ month _____ day

212*213*214

Steps towards the dream

★

지금 나에게 해주고 싶은 말은 무엇인가?

_____ year _____month _____day

_____ year _____month _____day

_____ year _____month _____day

215*216*217

Steps towards the dream

★

오늘 제일 처음 만난 사람은 누구인가?

_____ year _____month _____day

_____ year _____month _____day

_____ year _____month _____day

218*219*220
Steps towards the dream

★

오늘은 내게 어떤 의미인가?

_____ year _____ month _____ day

_____ year _____ month _____ day

_____ year _____ month _____ day

221*222*223

Steps towards the dream

★

함께 여행을 떠나고 싶은 사람은 누구인가?

_____ year _____month _____day

_____ year _____month _____day

_____ year _____month _____day

224*225*226
Steps towards the dream

★

지금, 후회하고 있는 일이 있는가?

_____ year _____month _____day

_____ year _____month _____day

_____ year _____month _____day

227*228*229

Steps towards the dream

★

미안하다고 말해 주고 싶은 사람이 있다면 누구인가?

_____ year _____month _____day

_____ year _____month _____day

_____ year _____month _____day

230*231*232

Steps towards the dream

★

나는 내일 _____ 하는 것이 두렵다.

_____ year _____month _____day

_____ year _____month _____day

_____ year _____month _____day

깊은 강물은 돌을 집어 던져도 흐려지지 않는다.
모욕을 받고 이내 화를 내는 인간은
작은 웅덩이에 불과하다

—

레프 톨스토이

233*234*235
Steps towards the dream

★

나에게 좋은 친구란 어떤 사람인가?

_____ year _____month _____day

_____ year _____month _____day

_____ year _____month _____day

236*237*238
Steps towards the dream

★

나는 비가 오면 ____하는 것이 좋다.

_____ year _____month _____day

_____ year _____month _____day

_____ year _____month _____day

239*240*241
Steps towards the dream

★

친구에게 들었던 가장 인상 깊은 말은 무엇인가?

_____ year _____month _____day

_____ year _____month _____day

_____ year _____month _____day

242*243*244
Steps towards the dream

★

나에게 삶이란 무엇인가?

_____ year _____month _____day

_____ year _____month _____day

_____ year _____month _____day

245*246*247
Steps towards the dream

★

나는 지금 어떤 삶을 살고 있는가?

_____ year _____ month _____ day

_____ year _____ month _____ day

_____ year _____ month _____ day

248*249*250

Steps towards the dream

★

누군가 내게 좋은 사람이라고 말했다면
어떤 점 때문이라고 생각하는가?

_____ year _____month _____day

_____ year _____month _____day

_____ year _____month _____day

251*252*253

Steps towards the dream

★

근래에 가장 큰 공감을 느낀 말은 무엇인가?

_____ year _____month _____day

_____ year _____month _____day

_____ year _____month _____day

254*255*256
Steps towards the dream

★

친구와 함께 했던 경험 중 가장 즐거웠던 기억은 무엇인가?

_____ year _____month _____day

_____ year _____month _____day

_____ year _____month _____day

257*258*259

Steps towards the dream

★

소중한 사람을 잃었을 때 어떤 생각을 했는가?

_____ year _____ month _____ day

_____ year _____ month _____ day

_____ year _____ month _____ day

260*261*262

Steps towards the dream

★

하나를 위해 모든 것을 포기할 수 있는가?
그렇다면 그것은 무엇인가

_____ year _____month _____day

_____ year _____month _____day

_____ year _____month _____day

여행에서 지식을 얻어 돌아오고 싶다면
지식을 몸에 지니고 가야 한다.

—

사무엘 존슨

263*264*265
Steps towards the dream

★

어릴적 내 꿈은 무엇이었는가?

_____ year _____month _____day

_____ year _____month _____day

_____ year _____month _____day

266*267*268
Steps towards the dream

★

나의 좌우명은 무엇인가?

_____ year _____month _____day

_____ year _____month _____day

_____ year _____month _____day

269*270*271

Steps towards the dream

★

노력해도 가질 수 없었던 것이 있었는가?

_____ year _____ month _____ day

_____ year _____ month _____ day

_____ year _____ month _____ day

272*273*274

Steps towards the dream

★

과거로 돌아간다면 하고 싶은 일은 무엇인가?

_____ year _____ month _____ day

_____ year _____ month _____ day

_____ year _____ month _____ day

275*276*277

Steps towards the dream

★

요즘 내가 가장 많이 하는 말은 무엇인가?

_____ year _____month _____day

_____ year _____month _____day

_____ year _____month _____day

278*279*280

Steps towards the dream

★

막연하게나마 도전해보고 싶은 것이 있다면 무엇인가?

_____ year _____month _____day

_____ year _____month _____day

_____ year _____month _____day

281*282*283

Steps towards the dream

★

오늘 하루 무엇이 나를 가장 즐겁게 했는가?

_____ year _____month _____day

_____ year _____month _____day

_____ year _____month _____day

284*285*286

Steps towards the dream

★

나에게 성공이 가져다 주는 것은 무엇인가?

_____ year _____ month _____ day

_____ year _____ month _____ day

_____ year _____ month _____ day

다른 동물들과 마찬가지로 인간도 환경으로 형성된다.
하지만 인간에게는 새로운 환경에 적응하거나
새로운 환경을 창조해내는 능력이 있다.

—

B.F. 스키너

287*288*289

Steps towards the dream

★

최근에 읽은 책 중 가장 기억나는 구절이 있다면 무엇인가?

_____ year _____ month _____ day

_____ year _____ month _____ day

_____ year _____ month _____ day

290*291*292
Steps towards the dream

★

나는 어떤 사람을 좋아하는가?

_____ year _____month _____day

_____ year _____month _____day

_____ year _____month _____day

293*294*295
Steps towards the dream

★

영화 속 주인공이 되고 싶었던 적이 있는가?

_____ year _____ month _____ day

_____ year _____ month _____ day

_____ year _____ month _____ day

296*297*298

Steps towards the dream

★

어렸을 적 꿈과 오늘날 꿈은 어떤 차이가 있는가?

_____ year _____month _____day

_____ year _____month _____day

_____ year _____month _____day

299*300*301

Steps towards the dream

★

지금, 나의 롤모델은 누구인가?

_____ year _____ month _____ day

_____ year _____ month _____ day

_____ year _____ month _____ day

302*303*304

Steps towards the dream

★

내가 도저히 참을 수 없는 것은 무엇인가?

_____ year _____month _____day

_____ year _____month _____day

_____ year _____month _____day

305*306*307

Steps towards the dream

★

부자가 된다면 하고 싶은 일은 무엇인가?

_____ year _____ month _____ day

_____ year _____ month _____ day

_____ year _____ month _____ day

308*309*310

Steps towards the dream

★

나를 동물에 비유하자면 어떤 동물에 가까운가?

_____ year _____ month _____ day

_____ year _____ month _____ day

_____ year _____ month _____ day

311*312*313

Steps towards the dream

★

내 방은 구체적으로 어떤 모습을 하고 있는가?

_____ year _____ month _____ day

_____ year _____ month _____ day

_____ year _____ month _____ day

314*315*316
Steps towards the dream

★

지금 가장 큰 고민은 무엇인가?

_____ year _____month _____day

_____ year _____month _____day

_____ year _____month _____day

317*318*319

Steps towards the dream

★

지난 한 해 동안 내게 일어난 가장 큰 변화는 무엇인가?

_____ year _____ month _____ day

_____ year _____ month _____ day

_____ year _____ month _____ day

320*321*322
Steps towards the dream

★

변화란 나에게 어떤 의미인가?

_____ year _____month _____day

_____ year _____month _____day

_____ year _____month _____day

자기 자신의 해낸 일을 즐기며

지금 하고 있는 일도 즐길 수 있는 사람이

행복한 사람이다

—

괴테

323*324*325

Steps towards the dream

★

외로울 때는 어떻게 하는가?

_____ year _____month _____day

_____ year _____month _____day

_____ year _____month _____day

326*327*328
Steps towards the dream

★

나에게 사랑이란 무엇인가?

_____ year _____month _____day

_____ year _____month _____day

_____ year _____month _____day

329*330*331
Steps towards the dream

★

지금, 사랑하는 사람이 있는가?

_____ year _____month _____day

_____ year _____month _____day

_____ year _____month _____day

332*333*334

Steps towards the dream

★

내가 좋아하는 단어, 색깔, 날씨는 무엇인가

_____ year _____month _____day

_____ year _____month _____day

_____ year _____month _____day

335*336*337
Steps towards the dream

★

지금 생각하는 사람의 이름과 느낌은 무엇인가?

_____ year _____month _____day

_____ year _____month _____day

_____ year _____month _____day

338*339*340
Steps towards the dream

★

어떤 사람과 결혼하고 싶은가? 혹은 싶었던가?

_____ year _____month _____day

_____ year _____month _____day

_____ year _____month _____day

341*342*343
Steps towards the dream

★

나는 어떤 부모가 되고 싶은가?

_____ year _____month _____day

_____ year _____month _____day

_____ year _____month _____day

344*345*346
Steps towards the dream

★

부모에게 느꼈던 상실감이 있다면 무엇인가?

_____ year _____ month _____ day

_____ year _____ month _____ day

_____ year _____ month _____ day

347*348*349
Steps towards the dream

★

나는 누군가를 사랑할 때, 어떤 변화들이 일어나는가?

_____ year _____month _____day

_____ year _____month _____day

_____ year _____month _____day

때로는 살아있는 것조차도 용기가 될 때가 있다.
—
세네카

350*351*352

Steps towards the dream

★

오늘 입은 옷의 색깔, 먹었던 음식, 있었던 장소를 기억하는가?

_____ year _____month _____day

_____ year _____month _____day

_____ year _____month _____day

Steps towards the dream

★

지금, 내게 필요한 위로의 말은 무엇인가?

_____ year _____month _____day

_____ year _____month _____day

_____ year _____month _____day

356*357*358

Steps towards the dream

★

지금 내가 하는 일은 만족스러운가?

_____ year _____ month _____ day

_____ year _____ month _____ day

_____ year _____ month _____ day

359*360*361

Steps towards the dream

★

첫 직장은 어떤 느낌일까? 혹은 어떤 느낌이었나?

_____ year _____ month _____ day

_____ year _____ month _____ day

_____ year _____ month _____ day

362*363*364

Steps towards the dream

★

시간이 없어도 꼭 시간을 내어 하는 취미가 있는가?

_____ year _____ month _____ day

_____ year _____ month _____ day

_____ year _____ month _____ day

365*366*367
Steps towards the dream

★

요즘 보는 즐겨보는 드라마는 어떤 내용인가?

_____ year _____ month _____ day

_____ year _____ month _____ day

_____ year _____ month _____ day

368*369*370
Steps towards the dream

★

만약 나의 미래를 미리 볼 수 있다면
언제의 나를 확인해 보고 싶은가?

_____ year _____month _____day

_____ year _____month _____day

_____ year _____month _____day

371*372*373
Steps towards the dream

★

내가 포기할 때라고 생각하는 순간은 언제인가?

_____ year _____ month _____ day

_____ year _____ month _____ day

_____ year _____ month _____ day

374*375*376

Steps towards the dream

★

나의 목표는 한결같은가?
아니면 때때로 전혀 다른방향으로 수정하는가?

_____ year _____month _____day

_____ year _____month _____day

_____ year _____month _____day

377*378*379
Steps towards the dream

★

기억나는 실수들이 있다면 무엇인가?

_____ year _____ month _____ day

_____ year _____ month _____ day

_____ year _____ month _____ day

젊음은 알지 못한 것을 탄식하고
나이는 하지 못한 것을 탄식한다.

—

앙리 에스티엔

380*381*382

Steps towards the dream

★

죽고 싶었던 순간이 있는가?

_____ year _____month _____day

_____ year _____month _____day

_____ year _____month _____day

383*384*385
Steps towards the dream

★

요즘 내게 부족한 것은 무엇인가?

_____ year _____month _____day

_____ year _____month _____day

_____ year _____month _____day

386*387*388

Steps towards the dream

★

나를 가장 즐겁게 해 주는 사람은 누구인가?

_____ year _____month _____day

_____ year _____month _____day

_____ year _____month _____day

389*390*391

Steps towards the dream

★

두 번 이상 읽은 책이 있는가?

_____ year _____month _____day

_____ year _____month _____day

_____ year _____month _____day

392*393*394

Steps towards the dream

★

힘든 순간 희망이 되는 것은 무엇인가?

_____ year _____month _____day

_____ year _____month _____day

_____ year _____month _____day

395*396*397
Steps towards the dream

배움이란 무엇인가?

_____ year _____month _____day

_____ year _____month _____day

_____ year _____month _____day

398*399*400
Steps towards the dream

★

혼자 울기에 알맞은 장소는 어디인가?

_____ year _____month _____day

_____ year _____month _____day

_____ year _____month _____day

401*402*403

Steps towards the dream

★

타인은 버리라고 하지만 버리지 못하는 물건이 있는가?

_____ year _____month _____day

_____ year _____month _____day

_____ year _____month _____day

404*405*406
Steps towards the dream

★

한 달 동안 나만을 위해 지출하는 돈은 얼마인가?

_____ year _____ month _____ day

_____ year _____ month _____ day

_____ year _____ month _____ day

407*408*409
Steps towards the dream

★

내가 한 거짓말 중 가장 기억에 남는 거짓말은 무엇인가?

_____ year _____month _____day

_____ year _____month _____day

_____ year _____month _____day

인간사에는 안정된 것이 하나도 없음을 기억하라.
그러므로 성공에 들뜨거나 역경에 지나치게 의기소침하지 마라.

—

소크라테스

410*411*412

Steps towards the dream

★

요즘들어 생긴 특이한 버릇이 있는가?

_____ year _____month _____day

_____ year _____month _____day

_____ year _____month _____day

413*414*415

Steps towards the dream

★

나는 크리스마스에 _____ 을 받고 싶다.

_____ year _____ month _____ day

_____ year _____ month _____ day

_____ year _____ month _____ day

416*417*418
Steps towards the dream

★

나는 얼마나 자주 부모님께 전화를 하는가?

_____ year _____month _____day

_____ year _____month _____day

_____ year _____month _____day

419*420*421

Steps towards the dream

★

복권에 당첨된다면 하고 싶은 일은 무엇인가?

_____ year _____month _____day

_____ year _____month _____day

_____ year _____month _____day

422*423*424
Steps towards the dream

★

지금 내 삶의 만족도는 얼마인가?

_____ year _____month _____day

_____ year _____month _____day

_____ year _____month _____day

425*426*427
Steps towards the dream

★

인생에서 전환점이었다고 생각되는 순간은 언제인가?

_____ year _____ month _____ day

_____ year _____ month _____ day

_____ year _____ month _____ day

428*429*430
Steps towards the dream

★

여행이 나에게 끼치는 영향은 무엇인가?

_____ year _____ month _____ day

_____ year _____ month _____ day

_____ year _____ month _____ day

431*432*433
Steps towards the dream

★

타인에게서 듣고 싶지 않은 말은 무엇인가?

_____ year _____month _____day

_____ year _____month _____day

_____ year _____month _____day

434*435*436
Steps towards the dream

★

그럭저럭 살아가기 위해 적절한 월급은 얼마라고 생각하는가?

_____ year _____month _____day

_____ year _____month _____day

_____ year _____month _____day

437*438*439
Steps towards the dream

★

지금 내가 받아야 할 상벌은 무엇인가?

_____ year _____month _____day

_____ year _____month _____day

_____ year _____month _____day

일의 기쁨에 대한 비밀은 한 단어에 들어있다.
그것은 바로 탁월함이다.
무엇을 잘 할 줄 안다는 것은 곧 이를 즐긴다는 것이다.

—

펄 벅

440*441*442

Steps towards the dream

★

나에게 어울리는 옷은 어떤 스타일인가?

_____ year _____ month _____ day

_____ year _____ month _____ day

_____ year _____ month _____ day

443*444*445

Steps towards the dream

★

내가 허영을 부릴 때는 언제인가?

_____ year _____month _____day

_____ year _____month _____day

_____ year _____month _____day

446*447*448
Steps towards the dream

★

나는 어떤 일을 할 때 가장 큰 능력을 발휘하는가?

_____ year _____month _____day

_____ year _____month _____day

_____ year _____month _____day

449*450*451

Steps towards the dream

나는 나의 의견을 분명하게 말하는가?

_____ year _____month _____day

_____ year _____month _____day

_____ year _____month _____day

452*453*454

Steps towards the dream

★

절대 용서할 수 없는 거짓말은 무엇인가?

_____ year _____month _____day

_____ year _____month _____day

_____ year _____month _____day

455*456*457

Steps towards the dream

★

하고 싶은 일을 실행하지 못하는 이유는 무엇인가?

_____ year _____month _____day

_____ year _____month _____day

_____ year _____month _____day

458*459*460

Steps towards the dream

★

양보하고 싶지 않은 일은 무엇인가?

_____ year _____month _____day

_____ year _____month _____day

_____ year _____month _____day

461*462*463

Steps towards the dream

★

살고 싶은 집은 어떤 형태인가?

_____ year _____month _____day

_____ year _____month _____day

_____ year _____month _____day

464*465*466

Steps towards the dream

★

자신감이 없을 때 하는 행동은 무엇인가?

_____ year _____ month _____ day

_____ year _____ month _____ day

_____ year _____ month _____ day

467*468*469
Steps towards the dream

★

실수로 인해 가르침을 얻은 적이 있는가?

_____ year _____month _____day

_____ year _____month _____day

_____ year _____month _____day

미래는 이미 시작되었다.

—

칼 융

470*471*472

Steps towards the dream

★

내 휴대폰 배경화면은 무엇인가?

_____ year _____month _____day

_____ year _____month _____day

_____ year _____month _____day

473*474*475

Steps towards the dream

★

나의 소망은 무엇인가?

_____ year _____month _____day

_____ year _____month _____day

_____ year _____month _____day

476*477*478

Steps towards the dream

★

혼자 있을 때 가장 많은 시간을 들여 하는 일은 무엇인가?

_____ year _____ month _____ day

_____ year _____ month _____ day

_____ year _____ month _____ day

479*480*481

Steps towards the dream

★

누구에게도 말하지 않은 비밀이 있는가?

_____ year _____ month _____ day

_____ year _____ month _____ day

_____ year _____ month _____ day

482*483*484

Steps towards the dream

★

책은 나에게 어떤 의미인가?

_____ year _____ month _____ day

_____ year _____ month _____ day

_____ year _____ month _____ day

485*486*487

Steps towards the dream

★

나의 인생을 책으로 쓴다면 제목은 무엇인가?

_____ year _____ month _____ day

_____ year _____ month _____ day

_____ year _____ month _____ day

488*489*490
Steps towards the dream

★

성장한다는 말은 무엇을 뜻하는가?

_____ year _____month _____day

_____ year _____month _____day

_____ year _____month _____day

491*492*493

Steps towards the dream

★

우연한 행운을 경험한 적이 있는가?

_____ year _____ month _____ day

_____ year _____ month _____ day

_____ year _____ month _____ day

494*495*496

Steps towards the dream

★

정리정돈과 나는 어떤 관계인가?

_____ year _____month _____day

_____ year _____month _____day

_____ year _____month _____day

497*498*499

Steps towards the dream

★

나는 계획적인 삶을 사는가?

_____ year _____month _____day

_____ year _____month _____day

_____ year _____month _____day

우리가 잘못된 길로 빠지는 것은
몰라서가 아니라 안다고 확신하기 때문이다.

—

마크 트웨인

500*501*502
Steps towards the dream

★

요즘 나의 가슴을 뛰게 하는 일은 무엇인가?

_____ year _____month _____day

_____ year _____month _____day

_____ year _____month _____day

503*504*505

Steps towards the dream

★

나를 당황하게 만든 사건은 무엇인가?

_____ year _____month _____day

_____ year _____month _____day

_____ year _____month _____day

506*507*508

Steps towards the dream

★

누군가를 울게 한 적이 있는가?

_____ year _____month _____day

_____ year _____month _____day

_____ year _____month _____day

509*510*511

Steps towards the dream

★

남을 도와준 경험이 있는가?

_____ year _____month _____day

_____ year _____month _____day

_____ year _____month _____day

512*513*514
Steps towards the dream

★

힘든 순간에 나를 이끌어준 사람은 누구인가?

_____ year _____ month _____ day

_____ year _____ month _____ day

_____ year _____ month _____ day

515*516*517
Steps towards the dream

★

여행 중 가장 편안하고 즐거웠던 동행자는 누구인가?

_____ year _____month _____day

_____ year _____month _____day

_____ year _____month _____day

518*519*520

Steps towards the dream

★

나는 _____을 봤을 눈물을 흘렸다.

_____ year _____month _____day

_____ year _____month _____day

_____ year _____month _____day

521*522*523

Steps towards the dream

★

나에게 청춘이란 무엇을 의미하는가?

_____ year _____month _____day

_____ year _____month _____day

_____ year _____month _____day

524*525*526
Steps towards the dream

★

나는 언제까지 살고 싶은가?

_____ year _____ month _____ day

_____ year _____ month _____ day

_____ year _____ month _____ day

527*528*529

Steps towards the dream

★

다시 태어난다면 어떤 사람이고 싶은가?

_____ year _____month _____day

_____ year _____month _____day

_____ year _____month _____day

절대 후회하지 마라.
좋았다면 추억이고, 나빴다면 경험이다

—

캐롤 터킹턴

530*531*532
Steps towards the dream

★

강인함이란 무엇인가?

_____ year _____month _____day

_____ year _____month _____day

_____ year _____month _____day

533*534*535

Steps towards the dream

★

내가 지금 가장 인내하고 있는 것은 무엇인가?

_____ year _____month _____day

_____ year _____month _____day

_____ year _____month _____day

536*537*538
Steps towards the dream

★

스스로가 작게 느껴질 때는 언제인가?

_____ year _____ month _____ day

_____ year _____ month _____ day

_____ year _____ month _____ day

539*540*541
Steps towards the dream

★

내가 만약 교사라면 어떤 과목을 가르치고 싶은가?

_____ year _____ month _____ day

_____ year _____ month _____ day

_____ year _____ month _____ day

542*543*544
Steps towards the dream

★

가장 기억에 남는 스승은 누구인가?

_____ year _____month _____day

_____ year _____month _____day

_____ year _____month _____day

545*546*547

Steps towards the dream

★

절대 변하지 않는 것이 있는가?

_____ year _____ month _____ day

_____ year _____ month _____ day

_____ year _____ month _____ day

548*549*550
Steps towards the dream

★

나는 언제 음악을 듣는가?

_____ year _____month _____day

_____ year _____month _____day

_____ year _____month _____day

551*552*553

Steps towards the dream

★

가족에게 가장 많이 하는 말은 무엇인가?

_____ year _____month _____day

_____ year _____month _____day

_____ year _____month _____day

554*555*556
Steps towards the dream

★

부모님께 나는 어떤 자식이고 싶은가?

_____ year _____month _____day

_____ year _____month _____day

_____ year _____month _____day

557*558*559

Steps towards the dream

★

스스로를 칭찬했던 순간이 있는가?

_____ year _____month _____day

_____ year _____month _____day

_____ year _____month _____day

나무를 베어 쓰러뜨리는데 한 시간이 주어진다면
나는 도끼를 가는데 45분을 쓰겠다.

—

에이브러햄 링컨

560*561*562
Steps towards the dream

★

오늘 만나서 얘기를 나눈 사람은 누구누구인가?

_____ year _____ month _____ day

_____ year _____ month _____ day

_____ year _____ month _____ day

563*564*565
Steps towards the dream

★

절대 주어진 시간 안에 끝나지 않을 것이라 생각되는 일이 있다면 어떻게 하겠는가?

_____ year _____month _____day

_____ year _____month _____day

_____ year _____month _____day

566*567*568

Steps towards the dream

★

첫사랑을 생각하면 무엇이 떠오르는가?

_____ year _____ month _____ day

_____ year _____ month _____ day

_____ year _____ month _____ day

569*570*571
Steps towards the dream

★

나를 어떤 모습으로 꾸미고 싶은가?

_____ year _____month _____day

_____ year _____month _____day

_____ year _____month _____day

572*573*574
Steps towards the dream

★

중요한 약속을 어긴 경험이 있는가?

_____ year _____month _____day

_____ year _____month _____day

_____ year _____month _____day

Steps towards the dream

★

나는 선택을 할 때 최우선으로 생각하는 것은 무엇인가?

_____ year _____month _____day

_____ year _____month _____day

_____ year _____month _____day

578*579*580

Steps towards the dream

★

내가 좋아하는 일과 현재 하고 있는 일에 차이점이 있는가?

_____ year _____ month _____ day

_____ year _____ month _____ day

_____ year _____ month _____ day

581*582*583
Steps towards the dream

★

내가 좋아하는 단어와 뜻은 무엇인가?

_____ year _____ month _____ day

_____ year _____ month _____ day

_____ year _____ month _____ day

584*585*586

Steps towards the dream

★

왜 사람은 누군가를 사랑하는 것일까?

_____ year _____ month _____ day

_____ year _____ month _____ day

_____ year _____ month _____ day

587*588*589

Steps towards the dream

★

사랑한다고 말해주고 싶은 사람이 있다면 누구인가?

_____ year _____month _____day

_____ year _____month _____day

_____ year _____month _____day

당신이 헛되이 보낸 오늘은
어제 죽은 이가 그토록 그리던 내일이다.

—

소포클레스

590*591*592
Steps towards the dream

★

특별한 사람으로 기억되고픈 대상이 있는가?

_____ year _____month _____day

_____ year _____month _____day

_____ year _____month _____day

593*594*595
Steps towards the dream

★

나는 건강한가?

_____ year _____month _____day

_____ year _____month _____day

_____ year _____month _____day

596*597*598

Steps towards the dream

★

내게 행복이란 어떤 모습인가?

_____ year _____ month _____ day

_____ year _____ month _____ day

_____ year _____ month _____ day

599*600*601

Steps towards the dream

★

구체적으로 그려본 미래의 나는 어떤 모습인가?

_____ year _____month _____day

_____ year _____month _____day

_____ year _____month _____day

602*603*604
Steps towards the dream

★

나를 가장 잘 아는 사람은 누구인가?

_____ year _____month _____day

_____ year _____month _____day

_____ year _____month _____day

605*606*607

Steps towards the dream

★

믿음이란 무엇인가?

_____ year _____ month _____ day

_____ year _____ month _____ day

_____ year _____ month _____ day

608*609*610
Steps towards the dream

★

자존심을 버렸던 순간이 있는가?

_____ year _____month _____day

_____ year _____month _____day

_____ year _____month _____day

611*612*613

Steps towards the dream

★

모든 것을 걸고 꼭 이루고자 했던 일이 있는가?

_____ year _____month _____day

_____ year _____month _____day

_____ year _____month _____day

614*615*616

Steps towards the dream

★

나는 왜 고민하는가?

_____ year _____month _____day

_____ year _____month _____day

_____ year _____month _____day

617*618*619

Steps towards the dream

★

답답할 때는 무슨 일을 하는가?

_____ year _____ month _____ day

_____ year _____ month _____ day

_____ year _____ month _____ day

성실함의 잣대로 스스로를 평가하라.
그리고 관대함의 잣대로 남들을 평가하라.

—

존 미첼 메이슨

620*621*622

Steps towards the dream

★

오늘 아침에 눈을 뜨고 처음 든 생각은 무엇인가?

_____ year _____month _____day

_____ year _____month _____day

_____ year _____month _____day

623*624*625
Steps towards the dream

★

누군가에게 오랫동안 말 못할 불만을 가진 적이 있는가?

_____ year _____ month _____ day

_____ year _____ month _____ day

_____ year _____ month _____ day

626*627*628

Steps towards the dream

★

나에게 최선이란 무엇인가?

_____ year _____month _____day

_____ year _____month _____day

_____ year _____month _____day

629*630*631

Steps towards the dream

★

나는 언제 최선을 다했는가?

_____ year _____month _____day

_____ year _____month _____day

_____ year _____month _____day

632*633*634

Steps towards the dream

★

나의 단점은 무엇이며 왜 단점이라고 생각하는가?

_____ year _____month _____day

_____ year _____month _____day

_____ year _____month _____day

635*636*637

Steps towards the dream

★

성공한 후의 인생은 무엇이 달라질까?

_____ year _____month _____day

_____ year _____month _____day

_____ year _____month _____day

638*639*640

Steps towards the dream

★

사람들은 잘 모르는 나의 잠재력은 무엇일까?

_____ year _____ month _____ day

_____ year _____ month _____ day

_____ year _____ month _____ day

641*642*643

Steps towards the dream

★

지난 밤 잠들기 전 떠올린 것은 무엇인가?

_____ year _____month _____day

_____ year _____month _____day

_____ year _____month _____day

644*645*646

Steps towards the dream

★

스스로 가장 매력적으로 느껴지는 순간은 언제인가?

_____ year _____ month _____ day

_____ year _____ month _____ day

_____ year _____ month _____ day

647*648*649

Steps towards the dream

★

꼭 지키고 싶은 것이 있는가?

_____ year _____month _____day

_____ year _____month _____day

_____ year _____month _____day

650*651*652

Steps towards the dream

★

나는 나를 믿는가?

_____ year _____month _____day

_____ year _____month _____day

_____ year _____month _____day

가장 큰 위험은
위험 없는 삶이다.

—

스티븐 코비

653*654*655

Steps towards the dream

★

좋아하는 계절과 날씨는 무엇인가?

_____ year _____month _____day

_____ year _____month _____day

_____ year _____month _____day

656*657*658

Steps towards the dream

★

나는 지금 누구와 살고 있는가?

_____ year _____month _____day

_____ year _____month _____day

_____ year _____month _____day

659*660*661
Steps towards the dream

★

다시 태어난다면 어떤 재능을 가지고 싶은가?

_____ year _____ month _____ day

_____ year _____ month _____ day

_____ year _____ month _____ day

662*663*664

Steps towards the dream

★

요즘 자주 가는 공간은 어디인가?

_____ year _____ month _____ day

_____ year _____ month _____ day

_____ year _____ month _____ day

665*666*667

Steps towards the dream

★

나는 외모에 많은 시간과 돈을 투자하고 있는가?

_____ year _____month _____day

_____ year _____month _____day

_____ year _____month _____day

668*669*670

Steps towards the dream

★

속마음을 털어놓는 친구가 몇 명 있는가?

_____ year _____ month _____ day

_____ year _____ month _____ day

_____ year _____ month _____ day

671*672*673

Steps towards the dream

★

자신의 실수를 남의 탓으로 돌린 적이 있는가?

_____ year _____month _____day

_____ year _____month _____day

_____ year _____month _____day

674*675*676
Steps towards the dream

★

마음이 답답할 때 가장 먼저 떠오르는 친구의 이름은 무엇인가?

_____ year _____month _____day

_____ year _____month _____day

_____ year _____month _____day

677*678*679
Steps towards the dream

★

가장 이상적인 휴식은 어떤 것인가?

_____ year _____ month _____ day

_____ year _____ month _____ day

_____ year _____ month _____ day

680*681*682

Steps towards the dream

★

스무 살의 나에게 하고 싶은 말은 무엇인가?

_____ year _____ month _____ day

_____ year _____ month _____ day

_____ year _____ month _____ day

절대로 고개를 떨구지 마라.
고개를 쳐들고 세상을 똑바로 바라보라.
—
헬렌켈러

683*684*685

Steps towards the dream

★

내일이 오늘과 달랐으면 하는 점은 무엇인가?

_____ year _____month _____day

_____ year _____month _____day

_____ year _____month _____day

686*687*688

Steps towards the dream

★

"내가 만약 너라면"의 너는 누구이며 무엇을 할 것인가?

_____ year _____ month _____ day

_____ year _____ month _____ day

_____ year _____ month _____ day

689*690*691

Steps towards the dream

★

가장 칭찬을 받고 싶은 대상은 누구인가?

_____ year _____ month _____ day

_____ year _____ month _____ day

_____ year _____ month _____ day

692*693*694
Steps towards the dream

★

지금 내 가방 속에 들어있는 것들은 무엇인가?

_____ year _____month _____day

_____ year _____month _____day

_____ year _____month _____day

695*696*697

Steps towards the dream

★

자존감이란 내게 어떤 의미인가?

_____ year _____ month _____ day

_____ year _____ month _____ day

_____ year _____ month _____ day

698*699*700
Steps towards the dream

★

내가 속해 있는 단체의 목적이 무엇인가?

_____ year _____ month _____ day

_____ year _____ month _____ day

_____ year _____ month _____ day

701*702*703
Steps towards the dream

★

두 번 다시는 일어나지 않았으면 하는 상황이 있다면 어떤 일인가?

_____ year _____month _____day

_____ year _____month _____day

_____ year _____month _____day

704*705*706
Steps towards the dream

★

내가 절대 할 수 없는 일은 무엇인가?

_____ year _____month _____day

_____ year _____month _____day

_____ year _____month _____day

707*708*709
Steps towards the dream

★

동경하는 직업은 무엇인가?

_____ year _____ month _____ day

_____ year _____ month _____ day

_____ year _____ month _____ day

710*711*712

Steps towards the dream

★

나를 항상 성가지게 한 것은 무엇인가?

_____ year _____month _____day

_____ year _____month _____day

_____ year _____month _____day

가장 오래 산 사람은 나이가 많은 사람이 아니라,
많은 경험을 한 사람이다.

—

찰스 다윈

713*714*715

Steps towards the dream

★

사랑하는 사람에게 했던 가장 후회스러운 행동은 무엇인가?

_____ year _____month _____day

_____ year _____month _____day

_____ year _____month _____day

716*717*718
Steps towards the dream

사춘기 자녀가 있다면 해주고픈 말은 무엇인가?

_____ year _____month _____day

_____ year _____month _____day

_____ year _____month _____day

719*720*721

Steps towards the dream

★

무인도에 꼭 가지고 가고 싶은 세 가지는 무엇인가?

_____ year _____month _____day

_____ year _____month _____day

_____ year _____month _____day

722*723*724
Steps towards the dream

★

마지막으로 편지를 쓴 대상은 누구인가?

_____ year _____ month _____ day

_____ year _____ month _____ day

_____ year _____ month _____ day

725*726*727
Steps towards the dream

★

하루 동안 초능력을 얻는다면 나는 어떤 능력을 가지고 싶은가?

_____ year _____month _____day

_____ year _____month _____day

_____ year _____month _____day

728*729*730

Steps towards the dream

★

어디에서 프로포즈를 받고 싶은가?

_____ year _____ month _____ day

_____ year _____ month _____ day

_____ year _____ month _____ day

731*732*733
Steps towards the dream

★

엄마에게 꼭 하고 싶은 말은 무엇인가?

_____ year _____month _____day

_____ year _____month _____day

_____ year _____month _____day

734*735*736
Steps towards the dream

★

지금 내 방에서 가장 불필요하다고 생각하는 것은 무엇인가?

_____ year _____ month _____ day

_____ year _____ month _____ day

_____ year _____ month _____ day

737*738*739

Steps towards the dream

★

나는 감성적인가? 이성적인가?

_____ year _____month _____day

_____ year _____month _____day

_____ year _____month _____day

740*741*742

Steps towards the dream

★

가장 좋아하는 영화는 무엇인가?

_____ year _____month _____day

_____ year _____month _____day

_____ year _____month _____day

경험은 창조할 수 있는 것이 아니라
반드시 겪으며 얻어야만 하는 것이다.

—

알베르 카뮈

743*744*745
Steps towards the dream

★

나의 이상형은 어떤 사람인가?

_____ year _____month _____day

_____ year _____month _____day

_____ year _____month _____day

746*747*748
Steps towards the dream

★

사후 묘비에 남기고 싶은 말이 있다면 무엇인가?

_____ year _____month _____day

_____ year _____month _____day

_____ year _____month _____day

749*750*751
Steps towards the dream

★

어린 시절 가장 재미있던 놀이는 무엇인가?

_____ year _____ month _____ day

_____ year _____ month _____ day

_____ year _____ month _____ day

752*753*754

Steps towards the dream

★

잠을 자는 동안 꾼 꿈 중에 가장 기억에 남는 꿈은 무엇인가?

_____ year _____month _____day

_____ year _____month _____day

_____ year _____month _____day

755*756*757

Steps towards the dream

★

나에게 졸업식은 어떤 느낌이었는가?

_____ year _____month _____day

_____ year _____month _____day

_____ year _____month _____day

758*759*760
Steps towards the dream

★

오랜 시간 결정을 내리지 못하고 미루고 있는 일이 있는가?

_____ year _____ month _____ day

_____ year _____ month _____ day

_____ year _____ month _____ day

761*762*763
Steps towards the dream

★

순간 이동을 할 수 있다면 지금 가고 싶은 곳은 어디인가?

_____ year _____month _____day

_____ year _____month _____day

_____ year _____month _____day

764*765*766

Steps towards the dream

★

내가 생각하는 영웅이란 무엇인가?

_____ year _____month _____day

_____ year _____month _____day

_____ year _____month _____day

767*768*769

Steps towards the dream

★

나는 지금 무엇을 쫓고 있는가?

_____ year _____ month _____ day

_____ year _____ month _____ day

_____ year _____ month _____ day

*770*771*772*

Steps towards the dream

★

부모님은 내가 어릴 적 어떤 사람이 되길 원했는가?

_____ year _____month _____day

_____ year _____month _____day

_____ year _____month _____day

오래 살기를 바라기 보다
잘 살기를 바라라.

—

벤자민 프랭클린

773*774*775

Steps towards the dream

★

버킷리스트 10가지를 적어보자.

_____ year _____month _____day

_____ year _____month _____day

_____ year _____month _____day

776*777*778

Steps towards the dream

★

오늘 하루를 색깔로 표현해 본다면?

_____ year _____ month _____ day

_____ year _____ month _____ day

_____ year _____ month _____ day

779*780*781
Steps towards the dream

★

하루 중 가장 행복한 시간은 몇 시인가?

_____ year _____month _____day

_____ year _____month _____day

_____ year _____month _____day

782*783*784
Steps towards the dream

★

오랫동안 고치지 못하고 있는 나쁜 습관은 무엇인가?

_____ year _____month _____day

_____ year _____month _____day

_____ year _____month _____day

785*786*787
Steps towards the dream

★

나만의 추억이 담긴 노래가 있다면 무엇인가?

_____ year _____ month _____ day

_____ year _____ month _____ day

_____ year _____ month _____ day

788*789*790

Steps towards the dream

★

가장 좋아하는 반찬은 무엇인가요?

_____ year _____ month _____ day

_____ year _____ month _____ day

_____ year _____ month _____ day

791*792*793

Steps towards the dream

★

나는 누군가를 위해 요리를 한 적이 있는가?

_____ year _____month _____day

_____ year _____month _____day

_____ year _____month _____day

794*795*796
Steps towards the dream

★

최근 가장 마음이 쓰이는 사람이 있다면 누구인가?

_____ year _____ month _____ day

_____ year _____ month _____ day

_____ year _____ month _____ day

*797*798*799*

Steps towards the dream

★

기억나는 노랫말이나 명대사는 무엇인가?

_____ year _____ month _____ day

_____ year _____ month _____ day

_____ year _____ month _____ day

800*801*802
Steps towards the dream

★

나는 얘기하는 것을 좋아하는가? 아니면 듣는 것을 좋아하는가?

_____ year _____ month _____ day

_____ year _____ month _____ day

_____ year _____ month _____ day

끊임없이 더 나은 사람이 되기 위해 노력하자.
여기에 인생의 참된 의미가 내재해 있다.

—

레프 톨스토이

803*804*805
Steps towards the dream

★

부적처럼 몸에 지니고 있는 물건이 있는가?

_____ year _____month _____day

_____ year _____month _____day

_____ year _____month _____day

806*807*808

Steps towards the dream

★

외출을 하기 위해 꼭 하는 것은 무엇이며, 얼만큼의 시간을 쓰는가?

_____ year _____ month _____ day

_____ year _____ month _____ day

_____ year _____ month _____ day

809*810*811

Steps towards the dream

★

최근에 들었던 말 중, 가장 기분 좋은 말은 무엇인가?

_____ year _____month _____day

_____ year _____month _____day

_____ year _____month _____day

812*813*814

Steps towards the dream

★

신체 부위 중 가장 자신 있는 곳은 어디인가?

_____ year _____month _____day

_____ year _____month _____day

_____ year _____month _____day

815*816*817

Steps towards the dream

★

1년 후의 내가 오늘의 나에게 하고싶은 말은 무엇일까?

_____ year _____ month _____ day

_____ year _____ month _____ day

_____ year _____ month _____ day

818*819*820

Steps towards the dream

★

나는 부모님께 먼저 연락을 하는 편인가?
마지막 통화는 언제인가?

_____ year _____month _____day

_____ year _____month _____day

_____ year _____month _____day

821*822*823

Steps towards the dream

★

맛있는 음식을 보면 가장 먼저 생각나는 사람은 누구인가?

_____ year _____month _____day

_____ year _____month _____day

_____ year _____month _____day

824*825*826

Steps towards the dream

★

올 해 가장 운이 좋았던 일은 무엇인가?

_____ year _____month _____day

_____ year _____month _____day

_____ year _____month _____day

827*828*829

Steps towards the dream

★

딸이 결혼할 때 해주고 싶은 말은 무엇인가?

_____ year _____ month _____ day

_____ year _____ month _____ day

_____ year _____ month _____ day

830*831*832

Steps towards the dream

★

요즘들어 가장 성실히 하는 일은 무엇인가?

_____ year _____month _____day

_____ year _____month _____day

_____ year _____month _____day

833*834*835

Steps towards the dream

★

나에게 집은 어떤 의미인가?

_____ year _____ month _____ day

_____ year _____ month _____ day

_____ year _____ month _____ day

해야 할 것은 하라.
모든 선행은 타인의 행복을 위해서인 동시에
나의 행복을 위해서이기도 하다.

—

레프 톨스토이

836*837*838

Steps towards the dream

★

처음 사랑을 느꼈을 때는 언제인가?

_____ year _____ month _____ day

_____ year _____ month _____ day

_____ year _____ month _____ day

839*840*841

Steps towards the dream

★

내가 바꿀 수 있는 것은 무엇이 있을까?

_____ year _____ month _____ day

_____ year _____ month _____ day

_____ year _____ month _____ day

842*843*844

Steps towards the dream

★

나는 지난 1년 동안 어떤 성장을 이루었는가?

_____ year _____ month _____ day

_____ year _____ month _____ day

_____ year _____ month _____ day

845*846*847
Steps towards the dream

★

사랑이 지칠 때는 언제인가?

_____ year _____month _____day

_____ year _____month _____day

_____ year _____month _____day

848*849*850

Steps towards the dream

★

나에게 이상적인 하루는 _____다.

_____ year _____month _____day

_____ year _____month _____day

_____ year _____month _____day

851*852*853

Steps towards the dream

★

나를 미워하는 사람에게 하고 싶은 말은 무엇인가?

_____ year _____month _____day

_____ year _____month _____day

_____ year _____month _____day

854*855*856

Steps towards the dream

★

주변에서 가장 행복한 사람은 누구인가?

_____ year _____month _____day

_____ year _____month _____day

_____ year _____month _____day

857*858*859

Steps towards the dream

★

행복하기 위해 필수적인 세 가지는 무엇일까?

_____ year _____ month _____ day

_____ year _____ month _____ day

_____ year _____ month _____ day

860*861*862

Steps towards the dream

★

만일 타인의 행복이 나의 불행으로 이어진다면 어떤 결정을 내리겠는가?

_____ year _____month _____day

_____ year _____month _____day

_____ year _____month _____day

863*864*865

Steps towards the dream

★

내게 이성 친구란 어떤 의미인가?

_____ year _____ month _____ day

_____ year _____ month _____ day

_____ year _____ month _____ day

무지를 두려워하라.
하지만 그보다도 더 두려워해야 할 것은
그릇된 지식이다.

—

레프 톨스토이

866*867*868

Steps towards the dream

★

최근에 가장 억울하고 분했던 일은 무엇인가?

_____ year _____month _____day

_____ year _____month _____day

_____ year _____month _____day

869*870*871

Steps towards the dream

★

자유란 무엇인가?

_____ year _____month _____day

_____ year _____month _____day

_____ year _____month _____day

872*873*874

Steps towards the dream

★

최근 가장 어이없는 사건은 무엇인가?

_____ year _____month _____day

_____ year _____month _____day

_____ year _____month _____day

875*876*877

Steps towards the dream

★

나는 어떤 자동차를 가지고 싶은가?

_____ year _____ month _____ day

_____ year _____ month _____ day

_____ year _____ month _____ day

878*879*880

Steps towards the dream

★

익숙해서 깨닫지 못한 소중함은 어떤 것이 있을까?

_____ year _____month _____day

_____ year _____month _____day

_____ year _____month _____day

881*882*883

Steps towards the dream

★

내게 친절을 베푼 사람에게 주고 싶은 선물은 무엇인가?

_____ year _____ month _____ day

_____ year _____ month _____ day

_____ year _____ month _____ day

884*885*886
Steps towards the dream

★

자주 가는 카페와 그 이유는 무엇인가?

_____ year _____month _____day

_____ year _____month _____day

_____ year _____month _____day

887*888*889
Steps towards the dream

★

내게 청춘은 언제인가?

_____ year _____month _____day

_____ year _____month _____day

_____ year _____month _____day

890*891*892

Steps towards the dream

★

요즘 아버지의 뒷모습을 보면 어떤 생각이 드는가?

_____ year _____month _____day

_____ year _____month _____day

_____ year _____month _____day

893*894*895

Steps towards the dream

★

꼭 가보고 싶은 공연이 있는가?

_____ year _____ month _____ day

_____ year _____ month _____ day

_____ year _____ month _____ day

무엇보다도 젊은 사람들이 스스로 무능력하다고 생각하며
실망에 빠지는 일이 없도록 해주세요.
먼저 자기가 무능력하다고 생각하지만 않는다면
사람은 누구 하나 무능력하지는 않을 것입니다.

―
펄벅

896*897*898

Steps towards the dream

★

좋아하는 스포츠는 무엇인가?

_____ year _____month _____day

_____ year _____month _____day

_____ year _____month _____day

899*900*901

Steps towards the dream

★

오늘의 스케줄을 확실하게 파악하고 있는가?

_____ year _____month _____day

_____ year _____month _____day

_____ year _____month _____day

902*903*904

Steps towards the dream

★

내가 잘 짓는 표정은 어떤 표정인가?

_____ year _____month _____day

_____ year _____month _____day

_____ year _____month _____day

905*906*907

Steps towards the dream

★

눈이 오면 하고 싶은 것은 무엇인가?

_____ year _____ month _____ day

_____ year _____ month _____ day

_____ year _____ month _____ day

908*909*910

Steps towards the dream

★

낭만적인 삶이란 무엇인가?

_____ year _____ month _____ day

_____ year _____ month _____ day

_____ year _____ month _____ day

911*912*913

Steps towards the dream

★

좋아하는 디저트는 무엇인가?

_____ year _____month _____day

_____ year _____month _____day

_____ year _____month _____day

914*915*916

Steps towards the dream

★

타인이 말하는 내 첫인상은 내 마음에 드는가?

_____ year _____month _____day

_____ year _____month _____day

_____ year _____month _____day

917*918*919

Steps towards the dream

★

이루지 못해 미련이 남은 사랑이 있는가?

_____ year _____month _____day

_____ year _____month _____day

_____ year _____month _____day

920*921*922

Steps towards the dream

★

죽기 전에 꼭 만나보고 싶은 사람은 누구인가?

_____ year _____month _____day

_____ year _____month _____day

_____ year _____month _____day

923*924*925

Steps towards the dream

★

나는 언제 지루함이나 무력함을 느끼는가?

_____ year _____month _____day

_____ year _____month _____day

_____ year _____month _____day

시간을 헛되게 하지 않는 것은 시간뿐이다.
—
르누아르

926*927*928
Steps towards the dream

★

내가 좋아하는 맛집은 어디인가?

_____ year _____month _____day

_____ year _____month _____day

_____ year _____month _____day

929*930*931
Steps towards the dream

★

내게 규칙, 규율이란 어떤 의미인가?

_____ year _____ month _____ day

_____ year _____ month _____ day

_____ year _____ month _____ day

932*933*934

Steps towards the dream

★

올 한 해를 한마디로 표현해 본다면?

_____ year _____ month _____ day

_____ year _____ month _____ day

_____ year _____ month _____ day

935*936*937

Steps towards the dream

★

신이 존재한다고 믿는가?

_____ year _____ month _____ day

_____ year _____ month _____ day

_____ year _____ month _____ day

938*939*940

Steps towards the dream

★

용기란 무엇인가?

_____ year _____month _____day

_____ year _____month _____day

_____ year _____month _____day

941*942*943
Steps towards the dream

★

나는 어디에서 살고 싶은가?

_____ year _____ month _____ day

_____ year _____ month _____ day

_____ year _____ month _____ day

944*945*946

Steps towards the dream

★

가장 마지막으로 눈물을 흘린 적은 언제인가?

_____ year _____month _____day

_____ year _____month _____day

_____ year _____month _____day

947*948*949

Steps towards the dream

★

술이 마시고 싶은 날은 언제인가?

_____ year _____month _____day

_____ year _____month _____day

_____ year _____month _____day

950*951*952

Steps towards the dream

★

지금 거울 속의 내 모습은 어떠한가?

_____ year _____ month _____ day

_____ year _____ month _____ day

_____ year _____ month _____ day

953*954*955

Steps towards the dream

★

기록은 나에게 어떤 의미인가?

_____ year _____ month _____ day

_____ year _____ month _____ day

_____ year _____ month _____ day

청춘이란 기묘한 것이다.
외부는 붉게 빛나고 있으나
내부에서는 아무것도 느낄 수 없다.

—

사르트르

956*957*958

Steps towards the dream

★

나는 어떤 직업을 가지고 싶은가?

_____ year _____month _____day

_____ year _____month _____day

_____ year _____month _____day

959*960*961

Steps towards the dream

★

가까운 지인이 세상을 떠난 적이 있는가?

_____ year _____month _____day

_____ year _____month _____day

_____ year _____month _____day

962*963*964
Steps towards the dream

★

나는 지금 누구와 어디에 살고 있는가?

_____ year _____ month _____ day

_____ year _____ month _____ day

_____ year _____ month _____ day

965*966*967
Steps towards the dream

★

내 삶에서 의식주를 제외하고 꼭 있어야만 하는 것은 무엇인가?

_____ year _____ month _____ day

_____ year _____ month _____ day

_____ year _____ month _____ day

968*969*970

Steps towards the dream

★

나에게 가장 큰 위기는 언제였는가?

_____ year _____month _____day

_____ year _____month _____day

_____ year _____month _____day

971*972*973
Steps towards the dream

★

오늘 하루를 향기로 표현해 본다면 무슨 향인가?

_____ year _____month _____day

_____ year _____month _____day

_____ year _____month _____day

974*975*976

Steps towards the dream

★

내게 주어진 사명이 있다면 무엇인가?

_____ year _____month _____day

_____ year _____month _____day

_____ year _____month _____day

977*978*979
Steps towards the dream

★

내가 가장 나답게 느껴지는 순간은 언제인가?

_____ year _____ month _____ day

_____ year _____ month _____ day

_____ year _____ month _____ day

980*981*982
Steps towards the dream

★

시간이란 내게 어떤 의미인가?

_____ year _____month _____day

_____ year _____month _____day

_____ year _____month _____day

983*984*985

Steps towards the dream

★

현재 내 모습을 상세히 표현해보자.

_____ year _____month _____day

_____ year _____month _____day

_____ year _____month _____day

986*987*988

Steps towards the dream

★

등산을 한 적이 있는가?

_____ year _____month _____day

_____ year _____month _____day

_____ year _____month _____day

989*990*991

Steps towards the dream

★

내가 예쁘고 멋지다고 생각할 때는 언제인가?

_____ year _____month _____day

_____ year _____month _____day

_____ year _____month _____day

992*993*994

Steps towards the dream

★

나는 무엇을 위해 돈을 벌어야 하는가?

_____ year _____ month _____ day

_____ year _____ month _____ day

_____ year _____ month _____ day

995*996*997

Steps towards the dream

★

오늘은 _____ 한 하루였다.

_____ year _____ month _____ day

_____ year _____ month _____ day

_____ year _____ month _____ day

998*999*1000
Steps towards the dream

★

30년 후에 나는 어떤 모습일까?

_____ year _____month _____day

_____ year _____month _____day

_____ year _____month _____day

인생은 한 권의 책과 같다.
어리석은 이는 그것을 쉽게 넘겨버리지만
현명한 인간은 열심히 읽는다. 단 한번 밖에
읽지 못한다는 사실을 알고 있기 때문이다.

—

상파울

Q&A to me
나를 찾아 떠나는 1000일

ⓒ 김민준, 2016

1판 1쇄 발행 2016년 1월 20일
1판 8쇄 발행 2022년 7월 20일

지은이 김민준
펴낸이 김해연
디자인 앨리스인드림
영업 남기성

펴낸곳 프로젝트A
출판등록 2013년 3월 14일 제311-2013-000020호
주소 03417 서울시 은평구 백련산로 14길 15 B02호
대표전화 02-359-2999
팩스 02-6442-0667
전자우편 haiyoun1220@daum.net

ISBN 979-11-86912-03-4(13190)

- 책값은 뒤표지에 있습니다.
- 잘못된 책은 구입하신 서점에서 교환해 드립니다.